# "Will I like it?"

# "Will I like it?"

Your first sexual experience: what to expect, what to avoid,
and how both of you can get the most out of it.

Written by Peter Mayle. Photographed by John Thornton.
Designed by Paul Walter.

WILL I LIKE IT?

Copyright c 1977 by Peter Mayle

Library of Congress Card No. 76-55145
ISBN 0-89474-005-9

*Manufactured in the United States of America*

Published by
CORWIN BOOKS
275 Madison Avenue
New York, N.Y. 10016

10 9 8 7 6 5 4 3 2 1

For Jennie.

# "Will I like it?"

# Great sexual expectations.

"...wave after wave of almost unbearable pleasure washed over them both, until with a final shattering orgasm they lay, spent and peaceful, in each other's arms as the first light of dawn came creeping through the window."

This extract is not, as far as we know, from any book that has ever been published. But it's the kind of highly romanticized sexual propaganda that you could find in hundreds of current novels. Authors turn their typewriters inside out attempting to describe the detailed sex life of their characters. And it is a firmly-held belief in mass-market publishing that you need a sex scene every twenty pages to keep the reader from falling asleep.

It's not a new idea, by any means. The Greek Gods and Goddesses described by Homer were always taking time off for a little sexual dalliance. Some of Chaucer's Canterbury Tales read like shooting scripts for a porno movie. Shakespearean characters fall in and out of love and bed with great regularity, considerable passion and a masterful control of the English language. The examples are endless.

Today, there's even more of it in evidence. Not just in books and plays, where it's always been, but in magazines, television and movies. Although so far, TV and most movies aren't as explicit in their sexual descriptions – the cut away to waves breaking on a beach, thunderstorms and sunsets still perform as visual substitutes for what we all know is going on in the bedroom.

And then, of course, there's advertising. Slim, perfect creatures with forty-dollar haircuts and wall-to-wall capped teeth invite us to share their cars, their meals, their liquor and their life style. If we do, maybe we'll have a perfect sex life, just like they have. A visitor from another planet, watching commercials for the first time, could easily think that a deodorant was some kind of earthly aphrodisiac, so rapid is its advertised effect on armpits and love life.

All this may sound as though we have something against sex. Far from it. The point we're trying to make is that a lot of sex, as advertised in books, plays, movies, TV and magazines, conditions us to expect sexual perfection. If our own first efforts don't measure up, we get disappointed and discouraged, and maybe even start to think there's something wrong with us.

There's nothing wrong at all, except that real life is seldom as well-organized as fiction.

Here's an example. We'll take the same sequence of events – man meets woman, they fall in love, they make love – and give you two different versions: as advertised, and something closer to reality.

THE FIRST TIME, AS ADVERTISED.

THE MEETING. It's a party. Everyone is good-looking, but our hero and heroine are undoubtedly the pick of the bunch. One is blonde, the other is dark – hoping to be mistaken for Robert Redford and Raquel Welch. Their eyes meet across the room, other guests make way as if by magic, and before you can grab a handful of peanuts, they are together in a secluded corner. Someone has thoughtfully turned the music down so they can talk to each other, but words are not necessary. They know. This is *it*.

FALLING IN LOVE. The time it takes is anything from thirty seconds (TV commercial) to around ninety minutes (feature movie). Our couple has a lot in common: those capped teeth, forty-dollar haircuts and photogenic features, for a start. Surprisingly, for two such handsome people, they came to the party unattached. Or perhaps their respective partners are falling in love off in another corner somewhere. Anyway, in less time than it takes to reload the camera, our hero and heroine have discovered that they are soul-mates. There is no doubt about what they're going to do next; the only question is where they're going to do it.

YOUR PLACE OR MINE? Her charming little apartment, or his house on the beach? It doesn't really matter. The sheets are clean, the dishes are done and the drinks are ready-mixed in both places. They leave the party and hop into his convertible, which is waiting, top down, right outside. (Parking problems, car thieves and bad weather are not permitted on these occasions.) A short ride, hair blowing in the breeze, a fifty-piece orchestra playing away in the back seat, and they've arrived.

BEFORE. As we suspected all along, there's a chilled bottle of wine ready, the view is spectacular, and the fifty-piece orchestra is installed out of sight but not out of hearing. One drink, a couple of kisses, and into the bedroom. Their clothes, which have obviously been checked out beforehand for stubborn buttons and sticking zippers, melt away, and there they are naked in the freshly laundered embrace of some fine king-sized percale. (You're probably wondering about room-mates. Shame on you. Our couple doesn't have roommates.)

DURING. Wow, what a pair. He is gentle and considerate, she is willing and passionate. His erection arrives right on cue, she moans in ecstasy, they know *exactly* what to do with each other. They both have explosive orgasms which occur, by a miracle of precision, at the same moment. And that's just for openers. With the staying power of two marathon runners and the agility of champion pole-vaulters, they make love again and again until, yes, there it is, dawn comes peeping through the window. This is the signal for a quick nap.

AFTER. Forty winks later, she's bustling around in his robe making coffee. Over the second cup, they are full of plans – none of which seem to include going to class or getting to the office on time. There's no embarrassment, no second thoughts, and no surprise that everything worked out so well. They knew it would the minute they saw each other. Besides, it was in the script.

THE FIRST TIME: ANOTHER VERSION.

THE MEETING. It is McDonald's, on a Saturday afternoon, and the usual glittering crowd is there; ketchup-smeared kids, harassed parents, and compulsive eaters hiding behind triple orders of French fries. He is making his way to a table when his foot slips on a fallen pickle, and half his chocolate shake spills over her Big Mac. It is aggravation at first sight, but at least they've met. After talking for half an hour, she decides she likes him enough to give him her phone number, which he writes on a paper napkin.

FALLING IN LOVE. Over the next few weeks, they get to like each other. She lives at home with her parents. He shares an old apartment with three friends. They're both students, both broke and both virgins. Sex is confined to kissing, and as much exploration of each other's bodies as they can manage with their clothes on. This becomes more and more frustrating. They reach the stage where they think about making it for real in the same way as a starving man dreams about a T-bone steak.

YOUR PLACE OR MINE? A problem. Her parents never seem to go anywhere. He's shy about getting his roommates to co-operate by leaving the apartment. (Can he trust them not to come back in the middle of everything? No. Will they want a blow-by-blow description afterward? Yes.) There must be a better place. But where? Hotels need money and nerve, and neither of them has a rich uncle with a spare penthouse. Eventually, opportunity comes along in the form of a 1971 Volkswagen, borrowed for a weekend from the friend of a friend. It's now or never.

BEFORE. The thought of what's going to happen travels with them like a back seat passenger. They drive out into the country, feeling that their intentions are written all over the car in three-foot letters. Finally, they reach the middle of nowhere and pull off the road. It's dark and cold, but at least it's private. This is *it*. Strangely enough, now that the moment has come, nervousness takes over from sexual desire. Yesterday they couldn't keep their hands off each other. Now they sit like strangers in the front seats. At last, overcoming the double obstacle of nerves and the stick-shift, they get close enough for nature to take over.

DURING. But even nature has difficulty when it comes to find-ing a position which encourages lovemaking. The reclining seats don't recline quite far enough; the car is suddenly full of handles and knobs that weren't there before. And clothes don't come off easily when the wearer is bent almost double. When they do come off, though, the unaccustomed feeling of skin against skin is fantastic. So fantastic that he comes after being inside her for only three or four strokes. He's embarrassed. She's upset. They're both bewildered. Is *that* what all the fuss is about? They get dressed.

AFTER. The drive back seems longer than the drive out. It's

We are all born virgins.

Sooner or later, out of love, sexual pressure or plain curiosity, most of us make love with another person, and are immediately disqualified as virgins.

This process is known as losing your virginity. And right there, almost before we've started, is an example of the misleading nonsense that has surrounded virginity for so long. How can you possibly *lose* something that requires deliberate and fairly accurate action by two people? You can give it, you can take it, you can share it, or you can keep it, but nobody we know has ever been careless enough to lose it.

It's an even stranger choice of words when you think of the importance that has been attached to virginity for thousands of years.

Even the Romans, inventors of the orgy and not noted for their upright morals, used to behave like Boy Scouts when they were around the Vestal Virgins.

A father, looking to make a good deal on the marriage of his daughter, had to accept a much lower price for the young lady if she wasn't delivered intact to the bridal bed.

And up until quite recently in some countries, proof of the bride's virginity was required after the wedding night in the form of a bloody sheet hung out of the bedroom window.

So virginity had a social, as well as personal importance, and to a certain extent still has. Fortunately, the days of treating a woman's virginity like a walking bank account or a trophy to be hung on the wall are over. The fact that young unmarried people make love is recognized. But even today, it's not fully accepted. There is still a considerable body of opinion that says: nice girls don't. (How ridiculous. If nice girls don't, how do they ever get to be nice mothers?)

Another absurd notion that has a good deal of support is that men should be experienced and women should be innocent. Apart from being patronizing to the female sex, it's also a mathematical impossibility. After all, it takes practice to become experienced, and it takes two to practice.

Nevertheless, the outlook for virgins today is better than it has been for years – there's no serious social stigma in changing your virgin status, the opportunities for doing so are abundant, and contraceptives are easily found. Thank your lucky stars; it was not always thus.

There's one basic factor which makes it unlikely that you will keep your virginity much past your late teens or early twenties, and that's your sex drive. It is a physical fact that from the end of puberty to early adulthood you are at your most sexually potent. Orgasms come thick and fast, and you are capable of a level of sexual activity that is exhausting even to think about when you get older.

This combination of minimum social restriction and maximum sexual pressure is difficult to resist. And why should you? Is virginity worth keeping?

The answer depends totally on you. If you have religious or moral beliefs that make you feel you should stay a virgin, then stay a virgin. Giving up your virginity against your better judgment will make you dislike yourself, your partner, and sex. Furthermore, it's something you can never get back. So if you have strong feelings against taking the plunge, don't. You won't enjoy it until you're mentally ready for it.

Even if you think you are ready, it's not something you should undertake casually one rainy afternoon when there's nothing else to do. Giving up your virginity is a sexual and psychological landmark in your life. It doesn't matter that it's happened to millions of men and women, and will happen to millions more. It doesn't matter that it's been happening for as long as life itself. For you, it's the first time, and it's important.

It's one of the very few occasions in your life that you'll remember, and the way it happens can often influence your attitude toward and enjoyment of sex for years afterward. Like anything you do for the first time, a little early success acts as a tremendous encouragement to try again; a first-time flop dampens your enthusiasm and withers your confidence.

But unlike almost anything else you do for the first time, there are no classes you can take. Nor is it easy to get any practical advice –

either before or after. Sadly, for something that is such a universal experience, very few people want to talk about it. And when they do, there is an even chance that what they say will be distorted by embarrassment ("It's awful; just one of those things we all go through") or highly exaggerated wishful thinking ("The first time I did it we both came 18 times").

For most of us, the truth lies somewhere in between the two extremes of disaster and triumph. Your first sexual experience is unlikely to be the most enjoyable one you'll ever have. On the other hand, it can and should be a lot of fun.

Difficult as it is to offer general hints that will apply to one of life's most personal events, that's what we will try to do in this book. But before getting down to some practical details, it is worth mentioning what is likely to be the biggest single barrier between you and your first enjoyable sexual experience: guilt.

Guilt is possibly the most effective and widespread sexual turn-off there is. It's been with us for thousands of years, and despite all the changes that have taken place in society and sexual convention, it's still with us today.

Why has it survived so long? One reason is the fear of being found out – and being found out in the most permanent way by the arrival of an unplanned baby.

The fear of producing a baby your first time out is a very valid one. You may hear stories about it being impossible for a woman to conceive during her first full sexual act, but they're mythical. Sperm and egg cells don't know about beginner's luck. If the time in the menstrual cycle is appropriate when you make love, a baby can result just as it can with a couple who have been making love for years.

Luckily, methods of contraception are now so varied and available that you have to be extremely careless to slip up. You'll find a list of all the major contraceptive devices, with comfort and safety ratings, later on in the book. And providing you take one or two very simple precautions, the thought of an unwanted pregnancy shouldn't interfere with your enjoyment.

The other part of the guilt barrier is not so easy to cope with, because it's a very basic feeling that many of us pick up during childhood and puberty. It's the idea that unmarried sex is wrong.

Maybe you're fortunate enough not to have any hangups about that, and your only strong feeling about sex is one of impatience to get at it. In that case, all we need say to you here is good luck, and hope that the rest of the book will give you some useful advice.

But for many of us, it's not that simple. Your body is saying go, but your mind is saying stop. There's a nagging worry that you *shouldn't.*

Why not? Is it going to hurt anyone? Is it going to make anyone unhappy? Is it going to make *you* unhappy?

If you can answer an honest "no" to those questions, you have nothing to worry about except worry itself; and that will pass when something stronger, like love or attraction, takes over.

Yes, giving up your virginity is important, just like any formative action in your life. But it's *your* virginity and it's *your* decision. If you want to share it with someone, you shouldn't feel guilty. Try to get rid of the idea that it's a big, mystical deal. It's not. It's just the start of your adult sex life. So start as you mean to go on – with enthusiasm, consideration and enjoyment.

The anatomy of a virgin.

To the outside world, virginity doesn't show.

If you're the only one in your group of friends who is still a virgin, you may feel conspicuous, but you won't look it. Similarly, on your first day as a non-virgin, you're going to feel very different, and it's almost impossible to believe that news of your first full sexual adventure isn't broadcast all over your face. But it's not. To parents, friends and the man behind the counter at the drug store, you'll look just the same.

However, virginity does have some very definite physical and emotional characteristics, and you should know about them.

Physically, it's impossible to distinguish the male virgin from his non-virgin brother. Nothing spectacular happens to the penis as a result of its first expedition into the vagina. There might be some soreness, which is usually slight and quite a pleasant souvenir of what has just happened. It may last for a day or two and is a very natural result of unaccustomed activity. Other than that, any male after-effects are confined to the emotions.

With women, there usually is a physical difference, which can sometimes create problems. It's called the hymen, and it lies in wait for unsuspecting lovers at the entrance to the vagina.

The hymen is a membrane which partially closes the entrance to the vaginal passage. To allow the penis in, this membrane has to be broken: this can be the act of a moment or a true labor of love, depending on its toughness. A really stubborn hymen can resist the attentions of even the most persistent penis, which is no fun for either of you. In this case, you have two alternatives. Either a gradual process of stretching by using fingers (yours or his): or a quick visit to the doctor. Even the toughest hymen can be surgically stretched or removed in a matter of minutes without going into a hospital – the doctor does it right there in his office. We're told it hurts about as little as having your ears pierced.

At the other end of the scale is no hymen at all. Many girls break their hymen quite accidentally, as a result of taking part in sports. Horseback riding in particular has accounted for the breaking of several hymens, which is hardly surprising when you consider the pounding it takes on the back of a horse.

If, despite an athletic childhood, your hymen is still intact, the chances are that it is fairly thin, and will give way at the appropriate moment without much discomfort. Even so, you should be prepared for some bleeding, and a wise virgin will keep a towel and a change of sheets handy for afterward.

### The emotional hymen.
The physical aspects of virginity may be fairly straightforward, but the mental side is a different story altogether.

Most of us, male and female, reach our early adulthood with a complex and often confusing set of attitudes about sex – a kind of emotional hymen made up of doubts and worries that develop along with our increased sexual consciousness. These are often mixed up with strong sexual feelings directed at either or both parents.

All this is absolutely normal; in fact, you'd have to be remarkably insensitive *not* to have some misgivings about the start of your sexual life. Everybody does. (Although not everybody admits to it.) So you can take some comfort from the knowledge that any worries you may have are not too different from the worries that millions of people have successfully overcome in the past.

It might help if we listed the most common doubts, worries and problems that combine to make up this emotional hymen. Some questions apply to one sex, some to the other, and some are common to both. Unless you're a professional worrier, you won't have anything like the full list, but your first partner might have some worries that you don't have. And since a happy sex life depends on mutual enjoyment, the more you know about your partner's feelings the better.

### Will it hurt?
Not unless you as a female have a super-tough hymen or a clumsy inconsiderate lover. In extreme cases, as we've said, a visit to the doctor will take care of the first problem; a few words in your lover's ear will help enormously with the second.

If he doesn't know already, for heaven's sake tell him you're a virgin. Keeping it a secret is pointless, and can actually turn the whole

occasion into a non-event. The surprise of discovering an unexpected hymen has caused many men to lose erections and confidence, both of which are basic requirements.

Once he knows that this is your first time, your lover should, if he's experienced, take the extra care and time necessary to prepare your vagina for his penis. The most pleasant way of doing this is for him to stimulate your clitoris and vagina with either his fingers or his tongue. That in itself will often give you an orgasm; if not, it should certainly start the flow of vaginal juices which will lubricate the passage and make the entry of the penis easier. To assist nature along, the most effective additional lubricant is saliva. If that doesn't appeal to either of you, keep some vaseline by the bed.

When both of you are virgins, you'll have to help each other find the way. There's no step-by-step manual for this; if what you're doing to each other feels good, then you're doing the right things. Try to take it slowly, and don't hesitate to tell each other what is giving pleasure and what isn't.

### Will I get an erection?

Your penis, which has been having erections for years, may suffer an attack of first-night nerves and let you down at the crucial moment. Don't despair. Any man can lose an erection, and all men do at one time or another. You're not impotent; just nervous.

Don't try to force an erection, because it won't be forced. Lie back, talk to your partner, relax. Concentrate on giving her as good a time as you can with your hands, mouth and tongue. The more involved you get in giving her pleasure, the quicker you'll forget about your temporary droop. And it is temporary. Once you stop worrying about it, your erection will return.

### Will I be frigid?

Just as men can go through temporary impotence, women can experience something which we'll call temporary frigidity – a lack of any sexual feeling at all during lovemaking.

Causes can be many and varied: fear of becoming pregnant, fear of intercourse being painful, a bad choice of time or place, or just not feeling in the mood. A woman's psychological and sexual make-up is more complicated than a man's, and can be affected by many more factors.

Very often, though, a woman will blame herself for being frigid when she should be blaming her lover for being incompetent. Even the most easily-roused woman isn't going to get much of a kick from a man who is clumsy, selfish and in a hurry with his lovemaking.

If you feel that your man could improve his technique and your mutual enjoyment, talk to him about it. He should be every bit as interested as you are in becoming a good lover.

True frigidity – where you have the right partner, the right setting, and no sexual worries that you can readily think of, yet you still feel nothing – is far too complex and personal to be handled in a book. It's something for experts to help with.

<u>Am I the right size?</u>

The size, shape and general disposition of the genital area is the subject of enough misinformation to fill a book on its own.

Here are the facts:

First, the vagina – a passage capable of almost unbelievable elasticity. Worries that it is too small are groundless; if it can expand to allow the exit of a baby, it can certainly handle the entry of a penis comfortably. The only times it can't are when the entrance is blocked by a hymen, or when the muscles in the vagina are tense and unyielding.

Happily, it is very rare for a vagina to be too large, either. Even if it is a more generous size than average, you can always achieve a pleasurable degree of tightness for both of you by experimenting with your lovemaking positions.

The clitoris, just above the vagina, varies in size, sensitivity and how erect it becomes. As far as we know, size has no bearing on sensitivity. The important thing is that you both know it's there and give it the attention it deserves. (Incidentally, there is a large and vocal school of thought which says that the clitoral orgasm is more intense and pleasurable than any other kind of orgasm. Maybe that will be true for you, maybe not. Try it.)

The size of the penis seems to be an eternal male obsession, beginning at infancy and probably reaching a peak around the time when you start sharing it with someone else in lovemaking. Penises do vary in size, but not nearly as much as you may think, and the variations are only really obvious in the resting position. When erect, the great majority of penises are about six inches long – just like yours. Size, in any case, has little to do with a man's ability as a lover; how you use what you have is infinitely more important.

### Will I come too fast?

Mainly a male worry. Women have the happy ability of coming again and again, often with hardly a break separating orgasms. Men usually need some time in between the last orgasm and the next erection. (Usually, the younger you are the less time you need.) The problem, of course, is that if the man comes almost instantly, the woman can be left aroused but unsatisfied – leading to disappointment and possibly three of the most deflating words a man can hear: "Was that *it?*"

Premature ejaculation, as it's called, like the failure to get an erection, is caused either by nervousness or over-eagerness. Since most men *are* nervous and over-eager the first time, it's no surprise that the lightning orgasm is a fairly common event.

What can you do about it? Masturbating half an hour or so before making love often helps; so does slowing down your stroke rate inside the vagina. If that doesn't work, console yourself with the knowledge that your next erection will probably be along in a few minutes, and this time you won't have quite the same irresistible urge to pop.

Meanwhile, console your partner. Your fingers, your mouth and your tongue can give just as much pleasure as your penis.

### Will I be a good lover?

Don't expect miracles. You have to learn to make love well, just as you have to learn anything more complicated than drawing breath.

But if you really want to be a good lover, you will be. You already have the necessary equipment. With the right partner, a considerate approach and plenty of practice, there's no reason why you shouldn't be terrific.

Try not to be influenced by bedroom athletes, who will tell you all the best lovers have a repertoire of 197 different positions. Nor by sexual computers, who tick up the number of orgasms with all the precision (and warm-blooded passion) of a taxi meter.

Find out what suits you and your partner. You're not out to please anybody else.

Will I enjoy it?

Yes. Making love has always been the world's most popular indoor sport. It wouldn't be so popular if it didn't feel so good.

For literally millions of people, the first time was the worst time.

That's one of the reasons why sexual problems are as widespread as the common cold. A bad start is something that can affect your sex life for days, weeks, months or even years. The more sensitive and self-critical you are, the longer it takes to pick yourself up and try again.

It's a particularly human complaint. Animals don't seem to suffer from sexual hangups unless they're penned up in captivity. (And if you had people peering at you through the bars of a cage, you'd find it tough too.) Under normal conditions, though, bears, apes, elephants, rabbits, horses – they all mate, as far as we know, without a moment's worry.

The difference between them and us, of course, is that we do worry about sex. More than that – we think about it, talk about it and agonize over it to such an extent that doing what comes naturally becomes far from natural.

We have to accept, as a fact of human nature, that we *do* think about it. Is there any way to make that thinking constructive and useful rather than anxious and self-defeating? We believe there is. While no amount of theorizing can take the place of experience, there is a positive approach toward sex which you, or anyone, can develop. It's partly your mental attitude, and partly your practical knowledge.

Obviously, one is affected by the other. The more you know, the less likely you are to worry when things don't go just right – because you'll know *why* they haven't gone right, and be able then to correct them. Curiously enough, the first and most important piece of sexual knowledge you should establish in your mind has nothing to do with the art or technique of lovemaking. It may sound obvious. It may seem simple. But it's the first mental step toward a relaxed enjoyment of sex in general, and your first time in particular. It's simply this: *you are not a special case.*

You may think that you have problems or doubts which are your *personal* anxieties and have never been experienced by anybody else before. It's not true. Every kind of misgiving you can possibly imagine, and many that you'd never think of, have been with us for centuries. The only reason they're not commonly known is that, until quite recently, nobody really talked about them. From genital size to bad breath – it's all been worried about long before you thought it up.

Not only have we had the same worries for generations, but we've made the same mistakes as well. And since learning from other people's mistakes is almost as instructive and much less painful than learning from your own, we thought it might be worth listing some of the more common ones. Here, then, is a collection of first-time blunders that have delayed the start of many a fulfilling sex life.

### The wrong reason.

Making love because you want to is one thing; making love because you feel you *ought* to is altogether different, and it usually ends badly. The trouble is that we tend to regard sexual inexperience as some kind of minor social disease. You get the feeling that there's something wrong with you – a feeling that is encouraged by people whose sexual ambitions run to quantity rather than quality. Their usual line is: "Why not? Everybody else does." Well, here's why not: unless you're genuinely attracted to the other person, you're unlikely to enjoy it much at the time, and you'll probably dislike yourself afterward. A misplaced feeling of social obligation is no substitute for sexual desire. And your next partner will have to cope with any after-effects left by your first cold-blooded experiment.

### The wrong partner.

The best definition that we've ever heard of the wrong partner is someone you'd hate to wake up with. By then, of course, it's too late to change your mind; but how were you to know? The only guidelines that make any kind of sense here are very, very general. For instance, do you *like* each other? (A completely different feeling from physical attraction or infatuation.) Do you have anything in common besides sex? Are you kind to each other? Would you be happy to go on spending time with each other if for some reason you couldn't make love? Can you talk to each other honestly about sex? The more no's you answer, the more you should think again. People don't change character when they take off their clothes, and it would put an impossible burden on the sexual side of your relationship if that had to compensate for everything else.

### The wrong place.

The wrong place is anywhere you can't relax. Some couples can (and do) manage beautifully in the middle of Central Park or in the back of a jumbo jet. Some couples actually find that the risk of discovery adds to their enjoyment. But these are probably tastes that take some time to develop, if at all. For most of us, sex is private, and even the thought of an audience is quite likely to halt the proceedings completely. Making love looking over your shoulder has never been a recommended position. Apart from anything else, it's uncomfortable, and discomfort can turn lovemaking into an obstacle course. If you're too cold or too cramped, you're going to miss half the fun. If your body is constantly being prodded by rocks in the ground, the hard arms of a chair, or the knobs that grow all over the inside of a car, it's difficult to enjoy yourself. Unless you'd be comfortable sleeping on it, don't try making love on it. Not the first time, anyway.

### Not enough time.

Lovemaking is a full meal that is too often treated like a snack. And if you once get into the snack habit, it can prevent you from discovering the rest of the menu. For couples who are making love regularly, a quick and uncontrolled session can be a stimulating change from leisurely lovemaking. But it's not the best introduction to sex, for a couple of very good reasons. First, a time limit is enough to make you nervous even if you weren't already, and you can certainly do without that. More important, if you restrict the time you inevitably restrict the enjoyment as well. Half an hour would be plenty if lovemaking were a simple matter of penis and vagina getting together, but it can and should be much more than that. A certain period of foreplay before actual coitus is usually essential for a woman. And the half hour or so of total relaxation immediately after orgasm is one of life's great luxuries. You should allow generously for both. The bedroom is no place for a stopwatch.

### Bad bed manners.

This covers a wide range of sexual sins, both large and small, and there's no good excuse for any of them. Dirt, for instance, is a profound turnoff. Greasy hair, unwashed genitals, and dirty finger and toenails are unpleasant and unnecessary. You're going to use your whole body when you make love: all of it should be clean. (Soap and water, incidentally, let you smell each other, whereas deodorants don't. Give the aerosols a rest.) Next, remember that your partner is probably as self-conscious as you are about your being naked together for the first time. Critical remarks about her breasts and vagina, or his penis, can either inhibit lovemaking or stop it completely. Laughter is even worse, if it's directed *at* one of you (not to be confused with laughing together, which is a great reliever of sexual tension). Something else to treat carefully the first time out is the smash-and-grab approach. If both of you feel like raping each other, fine. If not, an over-aggressive rush by either side can lead to an impossibly tense vagina or a lost erection. Finally, never underestimate the importance of the time just after you've made love. You're both vulnerable, and both anxious to hear some reassuring words. You need each other. If you were disappointed, or thought *you* were disappointing, don't sulk in silence. Be honest, and above all, be considerate. It shouldn't be too difficult; you like each other enough to be in the same bed.

Bad communication.

Neither of you is a mind-reader. You can't be expected to know by instinct what your partner likes or wants until you've had quite a lot of experience with each other. Some couples never find out. They spend their entire sexual lives without realizing what they could do for each other, simply because they never got into the habit of talking to each other. We're not suggesting you need to have a conference before you go to bed; but you should be able to tell each other what feels good. Just as important is being able to say what *doesn't* feel good; if your partner is doing something to you that leaves you cold then, as gently as possible, say so. Faking it in bed is a strain for you, and not much of a compliment to your partner, since it's a kind of dishonesty.

Did all that put you off? It shouldn't. You'll avoid 90% of the mistakes and problems we've touched on if your first sexual partner is someone you like, trust and can talk to. It sounds trite, but it's true: with the right person, you can have fun making love on a bicycle. With the wrong person, you could end up agreeing with Lord Chesterfield, whose feelings about sex were: "The enjoyment is quite temporary. The cost is exorbitant and the position is simply ridiculous."

It's up to you, obviously. All we can say before getting on to more positive suggestions is this – *if in doubt, don't.*

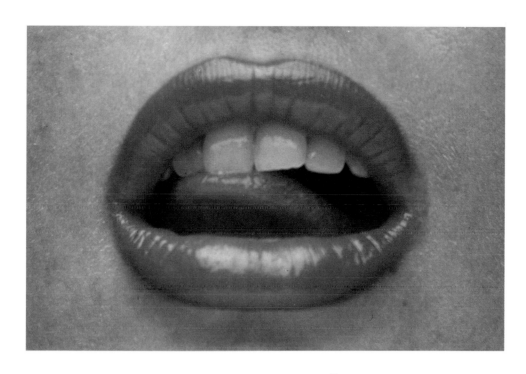

Doing it right.

The traditional idea of sexual initiation for young men was about as romantic as a package tour of Hoboken: a night out with the boys ending in a visit to the local whorehouse. As an introduction to sex, it was more often than not a disappointment. Prostitutes don't usually make very good partners, mainly because their hearts aren't in their work. Cash, not sex, is the reason they take up their profession, and the quicker you are in and out, the better they like it. (There are obviously some talented exceptions who take pride and pleasure in what they do, and charge top prices for doing it.) However, prostitution does at least offer some relief for those in need, and to that extent it's better than nothing.

Young women don't even have that. Perhaps the theory that nice girls don't also holds that nice girls don't even want to; just another part of the old sexual double standard that says boys will be boys, but girls will be ladies. Whatever the reasons, there is no freely available female equivalent to the brothel. Fortunately, times have changed, and society has recognized that women too have sexual appetites. Even so, women have less of a choice than men when it comes to taking their first sexual step.

For both men and women, there is an ideal way to start, which we include here more in hope than as a serious recommendation.

If you should meet someone who is kind, sexually experienced, preferably rich, usually older, and in love with you, make the most of it. (Always providing you want to.) A partner like that will make sure you get the ideal introduction to sex. If you've found one, skip this chapter. Your friend will teach you far more than any book ever will, and you'll enjoy every minute of it.

Failing that, you'll have to take your chances like the rest of us, and it is on this basis that the advice in this chapter is offered.

We've made three assumptions:
1. You are a virgin.
2. You have found the right partner – someone you like enough to make love with, and who attracts you enough so that you want to.
3. Your partner, if not a virgin, is still fairly inexperienced.

What now follows is *not* a collection of rules. Rules in sex don't exist. As long as you both enjoy what you do, you're doing fine. If you both find that you like sex in a candlelit room, or with spotlights on the bed; partly dressed, or naked; with mirrors, or without; in total silence, or with a stereophonic recording of a Harley-Davidson in third gear; whatever the surroundings, whatever the circumstances, if they give pleasure to both of you there's nothing wrong with them. The way you and your partner make love is your business.

So, bearing in mind that no generalizations can ever be more than rough guidelines, here are some practical hints. We've divided them into When, Where, How and Afterward, and we hope you find them helpful.

WHEN.

Some people swear that sex is best first thing in the morning. Others prefer the afternoon. In fact, clock time doesn't matter in the slightest – there is no magic hour of day or night when making love is any better than it is any other time. (The early morning theory is probably due to the fact that men often wake up with erections, but this is more likely the sign of a full bladder than virility.)

No, the only important thing to remember about time is that there must be enough of it, preferably several hours. You're both going to be nervous, and this can affect the way your genitals behave; the vagina may be dry and tense, or the penis may not become erect when it should.

On the other hand, it's just as likely that you'll both be so excited that you'll have orgasms in minutes, or even seconds.

Either way, it's vital that you give yourself enough time for a slower and more satisfactory replay. If at first you don't succeed, a sleep often works wonders, and you wake up fully aroused and ready for sex. If at first you succeeded too quickly, a break of an hour or so is all it takes to set you both up again – and this time you'll find it easier to hold back orgasm while you enjoy each other.

If you're having dinner together before going to bed, go easy on the food and drink. A huge meal is not the best way to start the evening – it makes you both feel heavy, and an attack of indigestion makes a poor bedmate. As for drink, it can be a small blessing, or a major disaster. A couple of glasses of wine will help to relax you, as alcohol tends to reduce your inhibitions. Too much, and you'll spend more time in the bathroom than the bedroom. For men particularly, alcohol increases desire but lessens performance, and is often to blame for lost or never-found erections (what the English sometimes call "Brewer's Droop").

We've always found that making love on an empty stomach is best. Furthermore, it makes the food you eat afterward taste delicious.

But that's a refinement. All you need to keep in mind at this stage is that your chances of a pleasurable start to sex are vastly increased if you can spend a good few hours together. Quite apart from any practical advantages, the feeling of waking up for the first time next to somebody you love is sensational. Don't miss it because you're in a hurry.

## WHERE.

What are the major alternatives?

Cars, with all their disadvantages, have enjoyed considerable popularity in the past because they were big, and easy to borrow. Now we're in the age of the compact and sub-compact, and what used to be uncomfortable has become almost impossible.

Beaches, fields, forests and parks give you more space to play in, but less privacy. Another snag: grains of sand, leaves, stones, twigs and pine-needles get everywhere.

We recommend bed, despite the difficulties that may be involved in finding one, for these reasons:

Privacy. A bedroom can protect you from the outside world almost completely. Take the phone off the hook, close the drapes if you want to, and you can concentrate on each other without worrying that a traffic cop will come and bang on the window half way through.

You may feel that your desire to make love to each other is too strong to be affected by thoughts of possible disturbance. Maybe it is. But maybe it isn't, and this first time is not the ideal moment to find out.

Warmth. An obvious, but often underrated part of lovemaking. Whether you do or not, you should always have the option of taking off all

your clothes without freezing. The whole of your body is there to be used and enjoyed, not just genitals, mouths and breasts. Cold hands and feet are uncomfortable for you and sometimes discouraging for your partner. (A breast or penis, when seized in an icy grip, often thinks of warmth before sex.) And goosebumps aren't very sexy.

In most bedrooms, you can regulate the temperature. Ideally, it should be warm enough for you to do without quilts and blankets, which are just another form of restrictive clothing. Snuggling up under a pile of bedclothes is fine after you've made love, but you don't want to be wrestling with them during the main event.

<u>Space</u>. A small bed is good; if you have the chance a big bed is better. When you're making love, you need room to maneuver freely without falling over the edge. You can't (even if you should want to) always restrict lovemaking to a space that measures 36" by 78".

A big bed is also better for sleeping afterward than the standard single, which tends to penalize the less bulky partner. For some reason – it can't be sexual, so it must be financial – most of the rooms in hotels and motels are equipped with twin beds. Dreadful things. If you have the nerve, insist on a double.

<u>Comfort</u>. This may sound like a middle-aged requirement for sexual happiness, but it matters. The more you can forget about outside distractions, the more you'll enjoy what you're doing. Bucket seats and sand dunes are no substitutes for a firm mattress and a couple of good pillows, and if you go the non-bed route your enjoyment may suffer accordingly. It's possible to make love almost anywhere on almost anything; even, according to some people, while standing up in a hammock. But who needs it? Stairs, chairs, tables and floors may become a part of your sex life in the future, when you've tried the more conventional delights. Until then, we suggest you stay in bed.

<u>Extras</u>. One last advantage of a bedroom is the collection of smaller comforts that are usually attached to it. First, the bathroom, filling the obvious needs, but also providing some hygienic pleasures. Taking a shower or bath together after making love is a great way to finish, and frequently a great way to start all over again.

Some more practical help you can give your lover is guiding him to your clitoris – it's sometimes not that easy for a man to find – and literally lending him a hand when the moment comes to take his penis inside your vagina. It will be a tight fit, and your hand, either opening the lips of your vagina or bringing his penis to exactly the right place, will make for smoother entry.

Two problems you might have to face, both due to nerves or inexperience, are the non-appearance of his erection or a very premature orgasm. The cure is the same for both: gentleness, understanding and patience, none of which is easy to give at the time. The erection will return sooner or later. How soon or how late depends very much on you, as there is nothing the man can do about it. (In fact, he's feeling worse than you are about his temporary loss of virility.) Your criticism will prolong the situation, just as your consideration will make it better. If your relationship is what it should be, the problem will be very short-lived.

<u>The man's side.</u> Far and away the most important three words in your head should be *don't rush it*. While both sexes can make this mistake, it's usually much more of a masculine fault, and there is a physical reason why this is so.

Men become sexually aroused more quickly and easily than women. It's quite possible for you to have an erection and an orgasm in minutes; long before the woman has reached the same pitch of excitement, sometimes even before you reach her vagina. It's frustrating for her, disappointing for you and, unfortunately, very common.

How can you stop it from happening to you? You can either try our suggestion of masturbating in advance. Or you can apply a basic self-discipline which is highly recommended anyway as part of lovemaking – postpone the moment of actually putting your penis in her vagina as long as you can.

Instead of your penis, use your fingers. Stretch the vagina gently (one finger, then two, then three). Alternate that with rubbing or tickling her clitoris, which you'll find with a little friendly guidance. After a while, you should feel the vagina becoming more moist as your partner becomes more excited. Keep this up until she has reached the same

Other extras, depending on the bedroom, are music if you feel like it; the choice of light, darkness or something in between; mirrors; TV (yes, some couples like the sound of voices without the risk of interruption); the chance to walk around naked; and finally, the knowledge that you can make a little noise without waking up the neighborhood.

Beds have only one disadvantage: they may be difficult for you to organize. If neither of you has an apartment, try to wait until a friend's place is available rather than go to a hotel or motel. Although the desk clerk won't ask for your marriage certificate, the business of registering may be more than your nerves can take. Also, you're likely to find those terrible twin beds. However, a motel bed is much better than no bed at all, and if that's the best you can arrange, check in and hang up the DO NOT DISTURB sign. P.S. Don't forget to take a suitcase.

<u>HOW.</u>
This is not a guide to sexual positions, although we include four favorites. Nor is it an advanced course on lovemaking. This is basic information – the sort of thing you should find useful during your first few hours of sex. We'll look at it from the point of view of each of you in turn.

<u>The woman's side.</u> You can't expect any man to know by instinct what pleases you and what doesn't. You'll have to show him, and the way that you show him makes a big difference to your mutual enjoyment.

It's not as complicated as it may sound, and at least part of it should come very naturally to you. If what he's doing turns you on, let him know it. That's simple enough. Not quite as simple is a tactful hint that he's doing something you don't enjoy – which could be anything from licking your toes to biting your neck. Just telling him to stop is sometimes enough of a discouragement to stop everything. It's better to steer him gently to a more pleasurable spot and tell him how good *that* feels. If he's half the man you think he is, he'll take the hint. This first time, you probably won't know what you like and what you don't until you try it, so you're both going to be experimenting. It's therefore difficult for us to be precise about any one detail. Just remember that an encouraging word in the ear is a major sexual stimulus for most men. If words fail you, actions won't, as long as you're really enjoying yourself. He'll get the message.

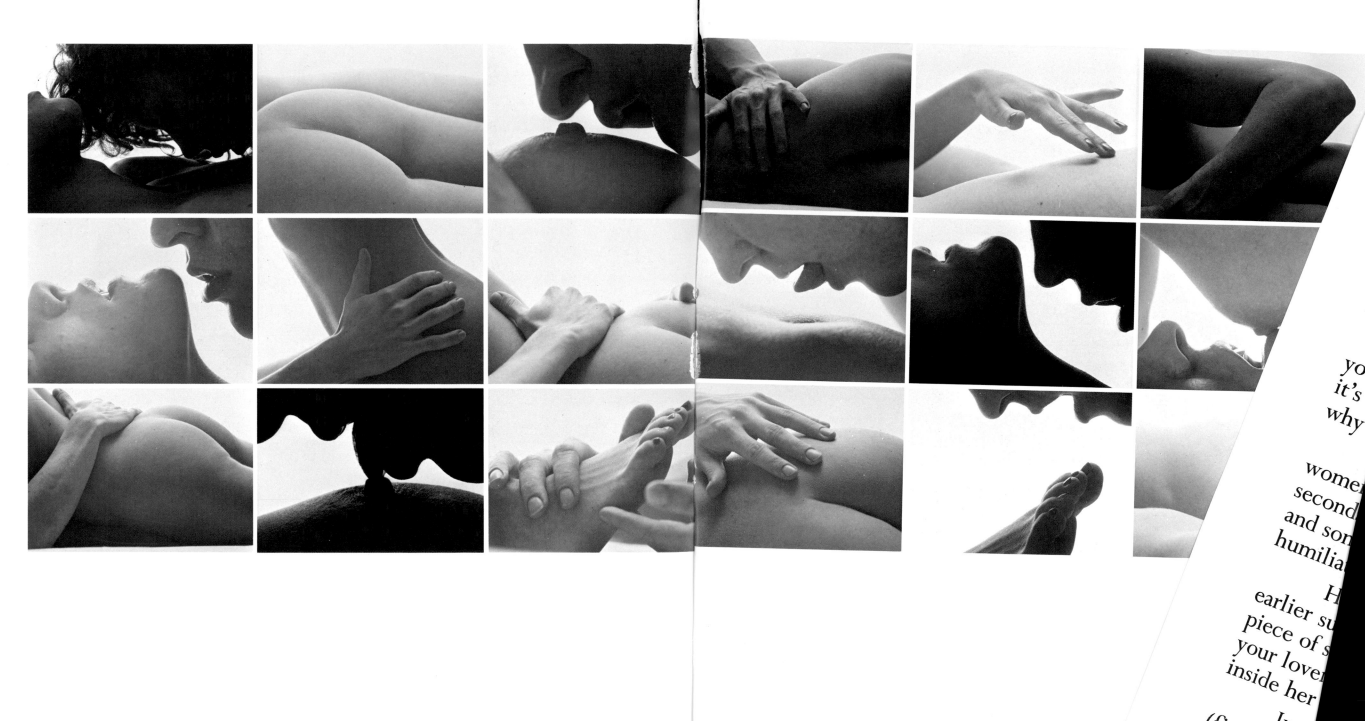

P
so
no
ab
situ
is w

your
it's us
why t

women
second
and son
humilia

H
earlier su
piece of s
your lover
inside her

Inst
(first one fi
licking her o
few minutes
partner becon

state of readiness as you. If she doesn't tell you – by words or by taking hold of your penis and bringing it to the entrance of her vagina – don't be afraid to ask.

Her vagina may or may not be very tight and difficult to enter; don't force it. Entering at the wrong moment is a painful and sometimes fatal turnoff. In stubborn cases that resist your combined efforts, a little vaseline on your penis and on the entrance to her vagina will help.

The feeling of being inside a woman for the first time is overwhelming, and unless you have superhuman control you won't be able to delay your orgasm for more than a very few minutes. You can't hope to stop it, but if you've spent enough time on the earlier part of your lovemaking, there's a good chance that she will come just as fast.

She might not, however, and you should be ready to help. Your penis may be temporarily out of action as a result of your orgasm, but there's nothing wrong with your fingers and tongue. Use either on her clitoris, just as you did before, until she is happy for you to stop. There's no excuse for leaving her up in the air.

Some positions. We've included four out of a possible one hundred and ninety-something. (Of which many are tiny variations that hardly count as separate positions. Besides, you won't have the time or energy for everything all at once.) Some will be better for you both than others, and you will develop your own variations anyway. But to start you off, try one or all of these.

1. *WOMAN-UNDER-MAN.* Although this position is the straightest one in the book, and although it comes in for a lot of criticism from the Women's Liberation movement and bedroom athletes, it has a good deal going for it.

Both of you are fully horizontal, with the man lying on top of the woman and between her open legs. (For a tighter fit, the woman can close her legs and the man open his.) The advantages are head-to-toe contact, good penetration of the vagina by the penis, stimulation of the clitoris by the man's pubic bone, and the fact that it's possibly the easiest position to slip into without too much thinking. Disadvantages are invented by sexual snobs, who jeer at it because it's simple and unsophisticated. Take no notice of them. You can both have as good a time in this position as you can in many more complicated ones.

2. *WOMAN ASTRIDE.* The man lies on his back, with the woman facing him, knees either side of his hips, feet tucked behind. From here, she lowers herself onto his penis. Excellent penetration, and it leaves both of you with free hands. Hers can be used on his chest, stomach, base of penis and (reaching behind) scrotum. His can reach her breasts, stomach, clitoris and buttocks. You don't get too much facial contact in this position, but it's good for most other parts of you.

3. *SIDE BY SIDE.* Lie on your side facing each other, with legs alternating: man's leg at the bottom/woman's leg/man's second leg/ woman's second leg. The penetration of the penis isn't as good as in position No. 1, but stimulation of the clitoris may be better. You also have head-to-toe contact, and one hand totally free (the other is usually round your partner's neck and shoulder). Movement is a little restricted, but that brings its own advantage by postponing orgasm. This position, because it takes some organizing, isn't one you should necessarily try the very first time – but it's something to remember for your second, more relaxed session.

4. *MAN BEHIND WOMAN.* As with other positions, this one has a long list of variations. Basically, it consists of the man entering the woman's vagina from behind, which means that she needs to kneel on all fours, or at least to be raised up by a pillow under stomach and hips. He then fits his penis through her legs and into her vagina. It's not what you would call a relaxed position, but the penetration can be very good. Whether that makes up for not seeing each other's faces, limited freedom of hand and body movement and the fairly strenuous movements involved is for you to judge. Once again, this is not recommended for absolute beginners, but it can be marvelous.

If you get around to trying those four basic positions during your first few hours, you'll be covering a lot of ground. Some of them may not appeal to you, in which case you'd be silly to attempt them. To begin with, stick to what sounds good and feels good. You'll develop you own variations if and when you're ready for them.

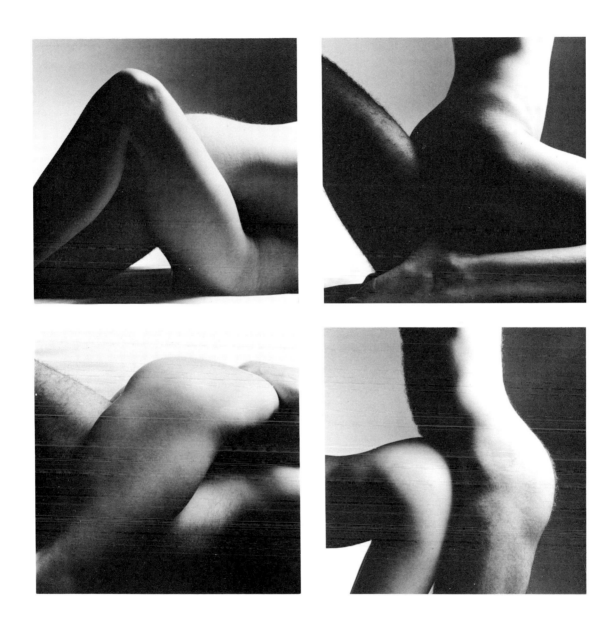

## AFTERWARD.

The period immediately after you have made love can be a joy to you both. Good sex gives you a feeling of physical well-being that is unlike anything else. And you're lying next to someone who means a lot to you. Who could ask for anything more?

Well, *you* could. You'll long for reassurance, especially the first time. You'll want to hear that you gave pleasure; that you were "good." You'll want affection, even though physical desire has been satisfied for the moment. And you'll want to feel it wasn't all a mistake.

Most of us need to hear and feel that way after we make love, including the person who is in bed with you. So if you had a great time, say so. If you feel tender, show it. Don't turn into strangers, when you've just been closer than friends.

And as a final act of consideration to your partner, don't go round telling the world you scored. It's childish and hurtful; tell someone you trust – it may be difficult not to – but no broadcasting. People are sensitive about things like that. So are you.

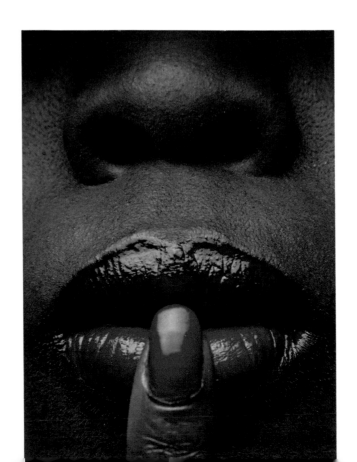

Suppose you prefer your own sex?

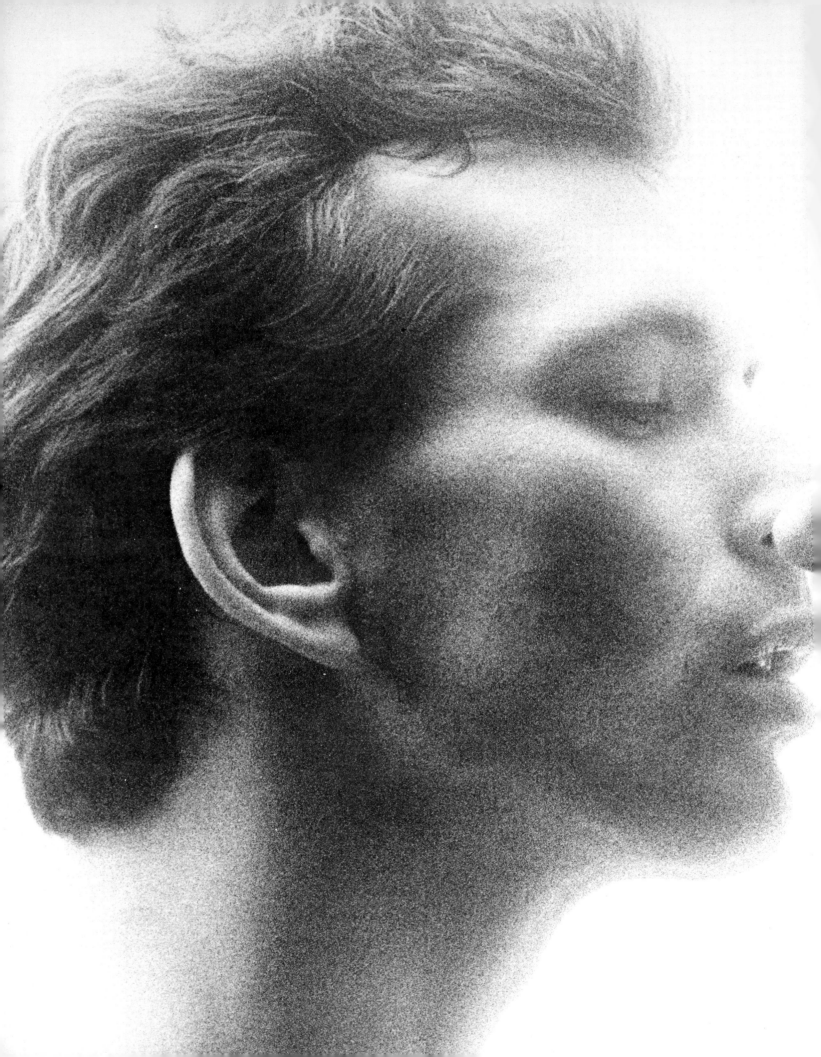

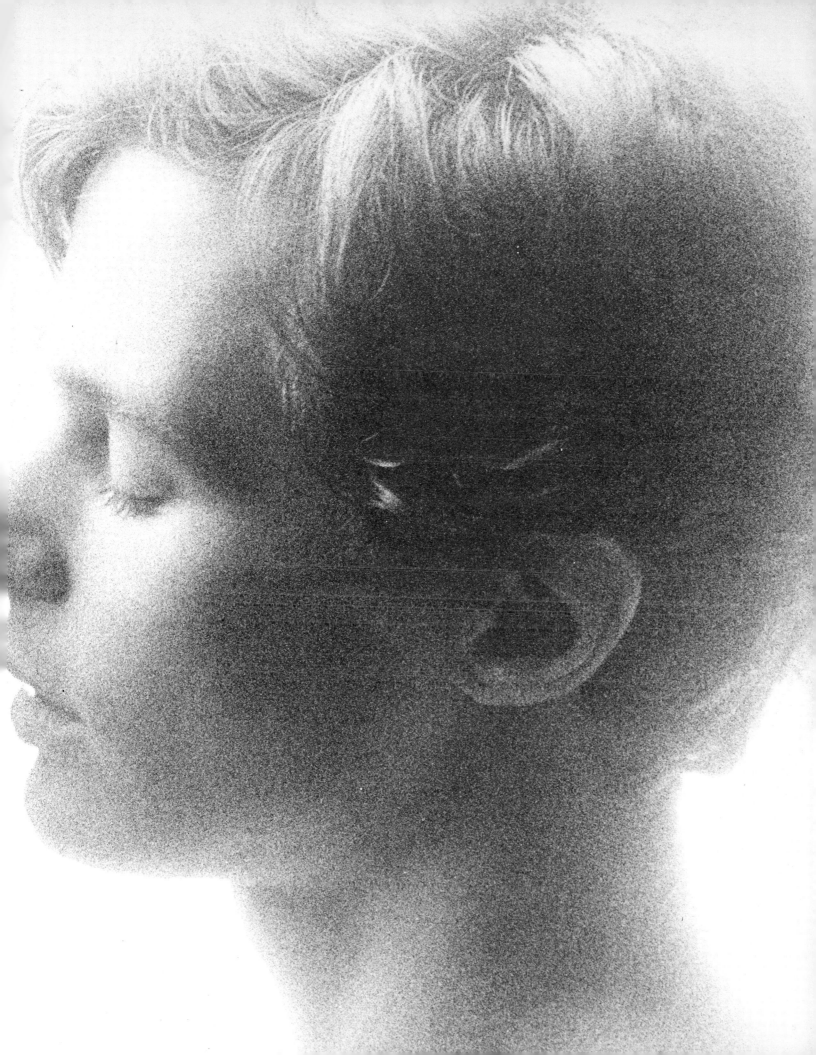

fighting men were, by our crude definition, homosexual: Pathan tribesmen in India, Greek and Japanese warriors and Roman legionaries have all been known to enjoy temporary or permanent preferences for their own sex.).

The female homosexual has to suffer the same kind of treatment, because she doesn't fit in either. She makes love for pleasure, not for breeding babies. And she doesn't need a man. In a family-oriented and male-dominated society, what could be worse?

You would think that society would have grown up more in its attitude towards the range of human sexual tastes, but apparently it hasn't. Despite Gay Liberation or any other signs of a more enlightened approach to sex, the old artificial division between people is still there: you're either "normal," or you're "odd."

This puts pressure on us all as we grow up to take sides, often before we know enough about ourselves to be fully ready. The easiest choice is always to go with the crowd, which in this case means being "normal." Hundreds of thousands of homosexual men and women have been pushed into that decision, and have suffered years of misery trying to be something they're not.

Because of the social pressure involved, it takes a great deal of self-confidence and courage to admit to homosexuality; it also adds to the difficulties of your first full sexual experience.

For one thing, your choice of potential partners is smaller. As far as we know there aren't any statistics on the subject, but it's fairly safe to assume that there aren't as many homosexual people in the world as there are heterosexuals. Even if, as is very likely, there are many more homosexuals around than you might think, they may not be prepared to admit it to you (or to themselves, for that matter).

Another problem: since homosexuality tends to be hidden rather than admitted, there are often none of the obvious signals of attraction and availability that exist in male/female relationships. Social events for young homosexual people don't exist. In practical terms alone, finding your first partner is made considerably more difficult when you step off the conventional sexual path.

It isn't easy to give advice about the emotional side of homosexuality without being homosexual. Perhaps one day there will be a generally available source of help for young homosexual people; it's certainly needed. All we can suggest here are some general thoughts based on observation rather than personal experience.

### Keep your options open.
Whether we like it or not, we live in a society that imposes sexual conditions on us – the chief one being that we must choose between one sex or the other. (Even though most of us would be able, in a less regimented sexual atmosphere, to enjoy both.)

You, like the rest of us, will make your choice. What you decide is obviously up to you, but try to wait until you know yourself well enough to be sure of what you're doing.

Remember that almost everyone goes through a homosexual phase at some time between childhood and full adulthood. It's a mistake to assume you're homosexual on the basis of occasional homosexual feelings, and it's a mistake to push yourself toward homosexuality because of them. Wait until you're sure, otherwise you could cause yourself a lot of unhappiness and confusion.

### Don't expect an easy time.
If you've made up your mind that homosexuality is the happiest option for you, be forewarned. There will unfortunately be some social penalties to pay unless you're very lucky.

Attitudes toward homosexuality may have changed for the better in the past few years. But sadly, they haven't changed that much. Homosexual men still have to cope with an unbelievable amount of intolerance and hostility which shows itself in dozens of different ways, ranging from name-calling to job discrimination. Lesbians may have a slightly easier time, but only because the prejudice against female homosexuality seems less violent.

However, both sexes will be made to feel different and uncomfortable from time to time; and that can be hard to take unless you're convinced that the sexual route you've chosen is the right one for you.

<u>Don't be ashamed.</u>

Much easier said than done, because of the indoctrination we all receive that says homosexuality is abnormal. (In terms of numbers, it's probably about as "abnormal" as being left-handed in a world designed for right-handed people. Normality in sex, anyway, doesn't exist, since the idea of what is normal varies so much from culture to culture, generation to generation, and person to person.)

Inevitably, you'll have doubts about your sexual self. Inevitably, you'll have periods of great confusion and lack of confidence. If it's any consolation, anyone who is at all sensitive and thoughtful goes through the same turmoil – homosexual and heterosexual alike.

Once you know that you would be happier with someone of your own sex, it's foolish to try to force your body and emotions in the other direction. They won't co-operate, and the results of suppressing your natural instincts will be miserable for you and anyone involved with you.

We say natural instincts, because for you that's what they are, despite what some out-dated attitudes or laws may say. Love and sex between two women or two men can be just as deeply-felt and mutually satisfying as anything the more conventional woman/man relationship can offer, with the obvious exception that it can't produce children.

Sex is a private matter for most of us. If you and your partner are giving and receiving pleasure from your relationship without hurting anyone, don't get hung up about what society thinks.

To quote the author Gore Vidal: "Sex of any sort is neither right nor wrong. It is."

Enjoy it.

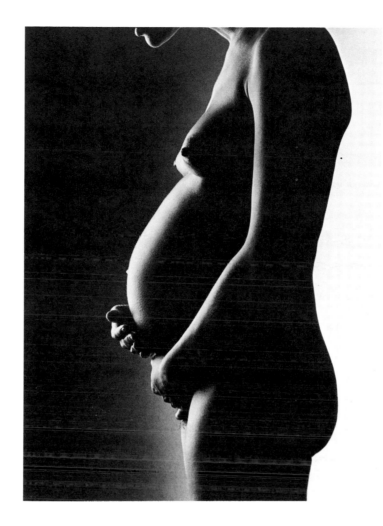

Don't start something you can't stop.

in the vagina before there's any chance of conception. Since it's impossible to be sure that simple washing has done the trick, most douches on the market contain a chemical sperm-killer. That in itself is often a reason to avoid the douche, as the chemicals may irritate the walls of your vagina.

Worse is to come, though. As the effectiveness of douching depends on you catching the sperm before the sperm catch the egg, speed is of the essence. In other words, you have to be out of bed and into the bathroom instead of enjoying one of the best parts of lovemaking – that marvelously relaxed feeling that comes immediately after orgasm.

Douching is better than nothing, but that's about the best you can say for it.

*Reliability:* poor.

*Suitability for first-time use:* an unromantic way to end what should be a romantic occasion.

*Comfort:* fine during lovemaking, lousy afterward.

THE CONDOM. Often, a man's first experience with contraceptives is with this thin rubber sheath worn over the penis. Old-fashioned it may be, but there's a lot to be said for it. It's easy, it's pretty reliable, and both of you know it's there.

Two possible disadvantages: the mechanical act of putting on a condom can interrupt your lovemaking. (On the other hand, if you do it together the process of rolling it on can be exciting for both of you.)

Also, a condom will obviously lessen the sensations felt by the penis. For those of you who come quickly, this can be a blessing; what you lose in sensitivity you gain in the time you can hold on before ejaculating.

Condoms are available in different thicknesses (the thinner they are, the more they cost), different colors, and with optional extras like fringes, bumps and ticklers. Whatever turns you both on.

As a general rule, the more decorative a condom, the less reliable it is, so be warned. Even less reliable are the cheap unbranded versions. Don't be tempted by the thought of saving a few pennies; it could turn out to be a very expensive form of economizing.

*Reliability:* very good.

*Suitability for first-time use:* good, specially as a form of visible reassurance.

*Comfort:* all the way from fair to excellent, depending on the sensitivity of your penis and the thinness of your brand.

THE DIAPHRAGM AND IUD. These are not of any immediate use to women who still have a hymen, as they are devices which need to be fitted inside you. But for future reference, here's how they work.

The diaphragm is made of soft rubber stretched over and around a flexible metal ring. It fits over the entrance to the womb, keeping the sperm from their hoped-for destination. Needless to say, if it doesn't fit well, you have problems. So if you ever decide to try a diaphragm, have it fitted by a doctor; and before using it in earnest, practice putting it in by yourself. All is in vain without accuracy.

Unlike the diaphragm, which you only wear when making love, the Intra Uterine Device is worn all the time. It can be made of plastic, nylon, stainless steel, or copper, and comes in different shapes: loop, spiral, star or T. It fits (and again, only a doctor should fit it) inside the uterus, and prevents the egg from being implanted. Reliability is excellent, with some reports putting it as high as 98% effective.

There are, however, serious drawbacks if you happen to be one of an unlucky minority. The IUD *can* cause peritonitis, blood clots, cramps and bleeding, urinary infections or growth of facial hair. Also, IUDs have been known to become displaced or fall out completely. It's only fair to say that these are alarming exceptions, and that about two million women in the U.S. find the device a comfortable, reliable and trouble-free companion.

As additional reinforcements, specially for use with the diaphragm, there are dozens of different sperm-killing jellies, creams and foams which you apply to the entrance to the womb before making love. They're chemical-based, and they're not completely reliable on their own, but they can provide a reassuring second line of defense.

*Reliability:* fair for the diaphragm, good for the IUD, but only if

properly fitted by a doctor, and checked for fit at regular intervals.

*Suitability for first-time use:* impossible with a hymen, and may be uncomfortable at first anyway. Also, the diaphragm requires pre-meditated action just before the event, and who knows when the event will come?

*Comfort:* can vary from unbearable to excellent, depending on how your body reacts.

THE PILL. Developed in the 1950's, and thus over its initial troubles, the Pill is probably the most generally suitable method. This is how it works:

Instead of attempting the risky business of trying to prevent the sperm and the egg from meeting each other, the Pill actually prevents ovulation (the release of the egg cell from the ovary). If there's no egg, there's no baby.

You take your first pill on the fifth day after the start of a period, then one a day for 20 consecutive days. Stop. One to three days after that, your next period should begin. On the fifth day, you start again. If that sounds like a mathematical exercise, it is. The reliability of the Pill depends on its regular and properly-timed consumption. But don't be discouraged; this can become as automatic a habit as cleaning your teeth.

The advantages of the Pill are obvious. Apart from its total reliability – except when you forget to take it – it doesn't interfere in any way with lovemaking. You don't feel it, your partner doesn't feel it, you don't have to stop to take it, and a month's supply takes up less room in your vacation baggage than a bikini.

The disadvantages are the side-effects that sometimes occur. Least serious, and perhaps most common, are a gain in weight and occasional feelings of nausea. Other problems can be much more severe. For instance: high blood pressure, blood clotting, pigmentation, blindness and cancer.

This is not intended to scare you, or to discourage you from using the Pill. Millions of women take it regularly without any adverse effects.

What we do want to emphasize is that the Pill is not something you fool around with. Get your doctor's advice before starting, and try what he or she suggests. If that doesn't work, and your first brand doesn't agree with you, go back for a change in prescription. There are plenty of different formulations, and you should be able to find one that suits you. But never, ever, be tempted to experiment on your own.

*Reliability:* excellent.

*Suitability for first-time use:* excellent. You don't have to worry about anything except each other.

*Comfort:* excellent. All you feel is relaxed.

VASECTOMY. Becoming more popular every year, this is a drastic but totally reliable male contraceptive. It requires a small surgical operation which closes off the tubes that carry sperm from the testicles to the penis.

No sperm – no babies. Ever. And that's the problem. Once you've had a vasectomy, you can't change your mind and therefore you can't ever have children of your own.

*Reliability:* total and permanent.

*Suitability for first-time use:* not recommended – why don't you wait until you've decided whether or not you want children.

*Comfort:* excellent.

ABORTION. This isn't the time or the place to get involved in the moral issues connected with abortion. It would be great if we didn't need to mention it at all. Unfortunately, despite all the methods of birth control currently available, accidents still happen.

Here, without taking any sides, are the basic facts about ending a pregnancy. We hope you will never need to know them.

If performed early enough – within the first three months of pregnancy – by a qualified specialist in a fully equipped clinic, abortion is no more dangerous or painful than any other minor operation.

After about three months, the operation is more complicated, and it is impossible to escape the fact that you are ending a life – even if it is an unborn life.

Whatever your feelings about abortion are now or may be later, one piece of advice will always hold true. Never, under any circumstances, go to a cheap, unqualified abortionist in some back alley. Hundreds of thousands of women do each year; thousands of them die, and others become sterile or seriously ill.

Don't risk it. A penny's worth of prevention is worth a thousand dollars' worth of cure.

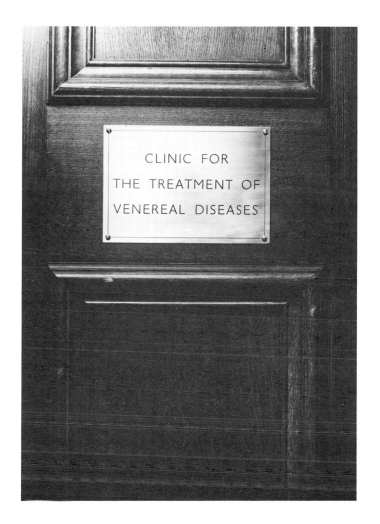

A cautionary chapter.

People would rather not talk about venereal diseases, and usually don't. It's an area of general sexual knowledge that is still surrounded by guilt, fear, shame, silence and ignorance – a combination which guarantees the continuing presence of VD in our society. If it were considered less of a sin, it would be easier to admit to, easier to treat, and would eventually disappear altogether. Since that hasn't happened yet, and isn't likely to, you'd better know about it.

Our first piece of misinformation about VD was a solemn warning that you could catch it from sitting on a lavatory seat. We believed it, and spent two or three uncomfortable and sometimes constipated years before finding out the truth. The way you catch VD is through sexual activity with someone who already has it. And not necessarily full sexual intercourse, either; you *can* catch syphilis from a kiss.

Another theory about VD is that it is largely spread by prostitutes. Probably not true – VD is bad for business, so prostitutes tend to be well informed about prevention techniques, and careful to use them.

Undoubtedly the best form of prevention is knowing your partner well enough to be sure that he or she isn't infected. Even that's not foolproof, so you should at least know the symptoms to watch out for. Here are the most common venereal complaints, starting with the worst.

SYPHILIS. This can literally be a killer if not treated quickly and professionally. Although it's sometimes very difficult to detect in women, the first sign is a hard sore which appears at the point where the germ has entered the body – usually the genitals. About seven to ten weeks after catching the disease, a more general rash develops on the skin, often combined with sores in the mouth and on the genitals. At this stage, syphilis is highly infectious.

Even without treatment, these symptoms disappear. But the disease doesn't. Sometimes after several years of inactivity, the third and final stage of syphilis takes place with horrifying results, including brain damage, blindness or heart disease. It doesn't even stop there. An unborn child can inherit syphilis from the mother.

The cure – if taken early enough and under medical supervision – is penicillin.

GONORRHEA. Also known as the clap, or a dose. Much less serious than syphilis, but very infectious and sometimes difficult to detect in women. The first symptom usually occurs a week or so after infection in the man, with a discharge of pus from the penis and a burning sensation when urinating. Female symptoms are similar – a discharge from the vagina and painful urination – but are often slower to appear, and sometimes aren't noticeable at all. Hence the difficulty in spotting the complaint.

Gonorrhea can be cleared up with antibiotics, taken under medical supervision. Do-it-yourself prophylactic kits are not reliable, and you shouldn't fool around with them.

Last and least, we come to a couple of minor disorders that don't really qualify as venereal diseases.

CRABS. The pubic or crab louse, which shelters in hair round the genitals or under the arms, can be caught from an unwashed partner. Cure is by powder or spray, according to doctor's recommendation. Prevention is a lot easier – crabs have a strong aversion to soap and water.

HONEYMOON BLADDER. Enthusiastic and prolonged lovemaking can sometimes leave the woman with a need to urinate much more frequently than usual. (Caused by the buffeting given to the bladder during intercourse.) If bleeding occurs, or there is pain, see a doctor. But don't worry about it; a few days rest will have everything back to normal.

PREVENTION. Short of sexual isolation, there is no way you can be totally sure of never catching VD. Increased sexual opportunity over the past few years, combined with a reluctance to get proper treatment, has caused VD to become very widespread; you probably know people who have it. There are, however, some simple precautions you can and should take. They don't provide complete insurance, but they help.

Know your partner. Sounds obvious, but many cases of gonorrhea are caught from "friends" who aren't friendly enough to be honest about their problem, or who don't even know they have one. If your would-be-partner has a discharge or sores, he or she would be better off with a doctor than in bed with you.

Visit the bathroom. Urinating after making love helps. So does washing thoroughly with soap. The most comfortable and efficient method of genital washing is the European bidet, a very civilized bathroom fixture which is not as popular as it should be in the U.S. Otherwise, use basin, bath or, for women, a douche.

Use a condom. (Or have him use one.) Apart from its usefulness as a contraceptive, the condom provides a measure of protection against VD. It's not the magic cure-all some people believe it to be, (it obviously can't, for instance, be expected to prevent the passing on of syphilis through kissing) but it is one of the best forms of prevention.

CURE. You and your partner may know all there is to know about VD; both of you may take every possible precaution. And, despite everything, you may still have the bad luck to catch it in one form or another.

The worst thing you can do is keep quiet and hope it will go away. It won't. And in the case of syphilis, head-in-the-sand behavior will have severe and long-lasting results on you and possibly your children.

There's no easy way out. If you think you have VD, *you must see a doctor.* Pretending you don't have VD, and refusing to have it treated, is anti-social and potentially dangerous. Self-treatment is unreliable at the best of times, and some quack remedies are extremely harmful. There is absolutely no substitute for qualified medical advice and treatment.

Your regular doctor is the best person to see, because you can get an appointment and begin treatment very quickly. (And the sooner VD is treated, the quicker it's cured.) You needn't feel you're a special case; he or she has probably treated hundreds of people with VD. If it really is too difficult and embarrassing for you to visit your own doctor, you might prefer the less personal atmosphere of a hospital clinic where nobody knows you. They aren't the most pleasant places to be, but it may be easier for you than admitting VD to the family doctor, who is often also a family friend. To find a VD clinic, call up hospitals in the area where you live. Most good-sized towns have one.

While you're waiting for treatment to begin, and when you're being

treated, avoid having sex. You'll only be passing on your misfortune to someone else.

Finally, if you have even the slightest suspicion that you've caught something, have the decency to tell your partner. He or she has a right to know anyway, and the problem will be easier to cope with if it's shared between you.

VD is only dangerous when it remains secret and untreated. That *is* something to feel guilty about. Catching it in the first place is just rotten luck.